Electricity

Words by Mark W. Bailey

Professional Engineer
Commonwealth Edison Company

Raintree Childrens Books
Milwaukee • Toronto • Melbourne • London

Library of Congress Number: 77-27324

6 7 8 9 0 85 84 83

Printed and bound in the United States of America.

Library of Congress Cataloging in Publication Data

Bailey, Mark W.
    Electricity.

    (Read about)
    Bibliography: p.
    Includes index.
    SUMMARY: Discusses different ways of producing
and using electricity.
    1.   Electricity — Juvenile literature.   [1.   Elec-
tricity]   I.   Title.
QC527.2.M67   537   77-27324
ISBN 0-8393-0085-9 lib. bdg.

Electricity

What do you do when it gets dark in the
house? You turn on a light. You just turn
on a switch, and it isn't dark anymore.
There are many different kinds of lamps.
You can have table lamps, wall lamps, floor
lamps, and overhead lamps. All these lamps
use electricity to give light.

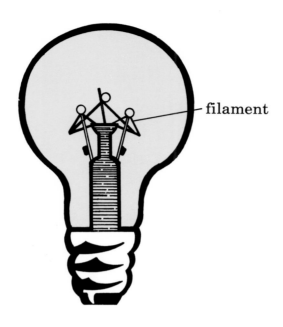

filament

It seems like magic, but it isn't. Lamps hold light bulbs. When you turn on a light switch, electricity comes through a wire to the light bulb. Inside the light bulb is a thin piece of wire called a filament. The electricity heats the filament. Then it gets hot and glows. That is what makes the light.

Some lamps are in a wall or a ceiling. They can be turned on by a switch on the wall. Table lamps do not use wall switches. They have their own switch. They also have a cord. The cord goes into a wall outlet. In the outlet there is electricity. When the lamp switch is turned on, the electricity goes to the filament in the light bulb.

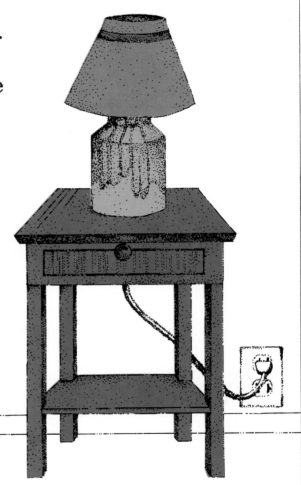

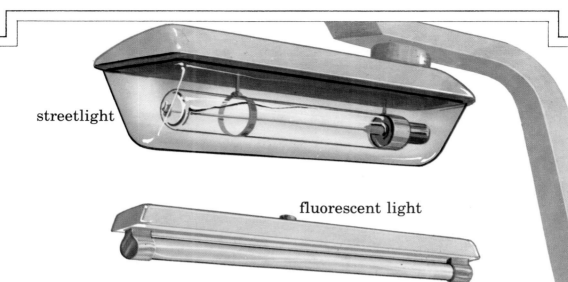

streetlight

fluorescent light

Another kind of electric light is a gas discharge lamp. It does not have a filament. It has a gas inside. Electricity makes the gas glow.

There are two kinds of gas discharge lamps. One kind is often in a kitchen or a bathroom. It is called a fluorescent light. Fluorescent lights are painted on the inside with a special paint. The paint gives the light from the fluorescent bulb a bright white glow.

The second kind of gas discharge lamp is used for streetlights. These lights are not painted on the inside. Their light looks like daylight.

Electricity can be used to run many things in your house. How many can you see?

The appliances in your house get electricity from wires. The wires are in the walls. The wires are in a pipe called a conduit. It is made of aluminum and steel. Electricity can make wires very hot. The conduit protects the walls from the hot wires.

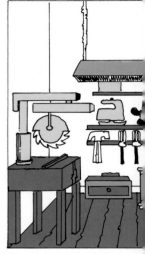

All of these wires come together in one place. They come together at the meter. The meter is where electricity comes into the house.

cord

meter

socket

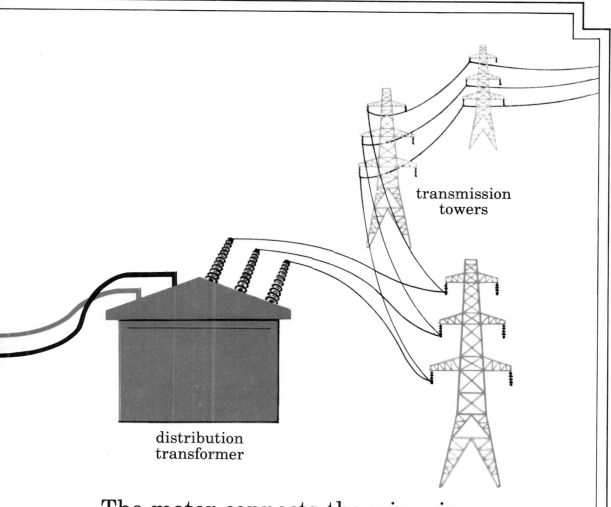

transmission
towers

distribution
transformer

The meter connects the wires in your
house to a distribution transformer outside
your house.

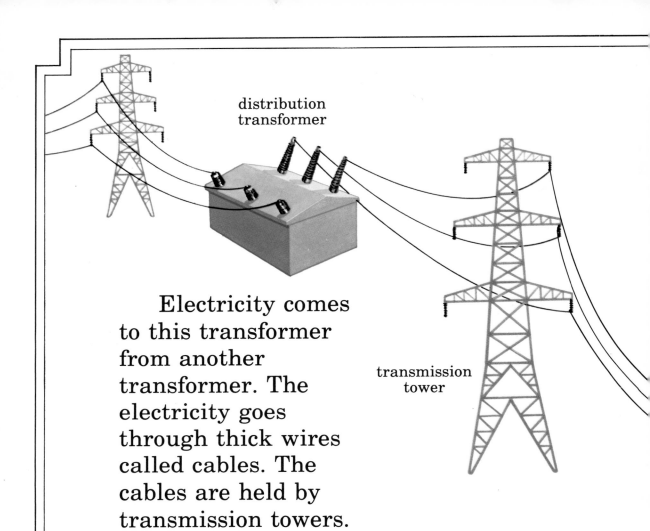

distribution
transformer

transmission
tower

Electricity comes to this transformer from another transformer. The electricity goes through thick wires called cables. The cables are held by transmission towers.

The cables bring electricity from a power station. Electricity is made in the power station.

distribution transformer

cooling towers

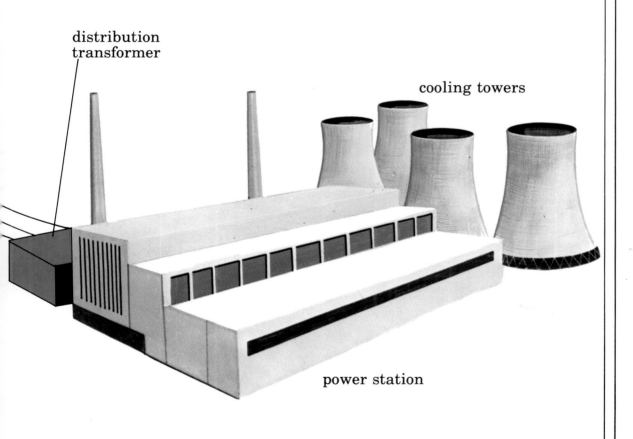

power station

13

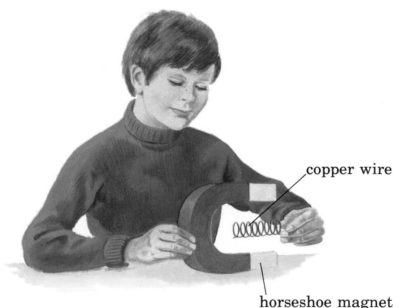

copper wire

horseshoe magnet

How is electricity made? It can be made by using a horseshoe magnet and a coil of copper wire. If you pass a copper coil between the ends of the magnet, electricity will be made in the coil. Electricity is one kind of energy.

You will know electricity is in the coil if it makes something work.

light bulb

This boy has made a simple dynamo. A dynamo is a machine that makes electricity.

The dynamo has a handle attached to some copper wire. The copper wire is between the ends of a horseshoe magnet. When a boy turns the handle, the wire turns around. This makes enough electricity to light a light bulb.

There is another way to make a dynamo. Put a bar magnet on the end of the handle. Then put a coil of copper wire around the bar magnet. When you turn the handle, the bar magnet will turn. That makes electricity.

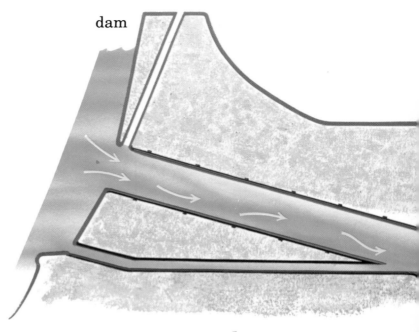

dam

There are many ways to make a
dynamo work. Some power stations use
water to make electricity. This kind of
electricity is called hydroelectricity. Hydro
means water.

Water is held behind a dam. When the
dam is opened, the water rushes down a big
pipe. At the end of the pipe is a big turbine
wheel.

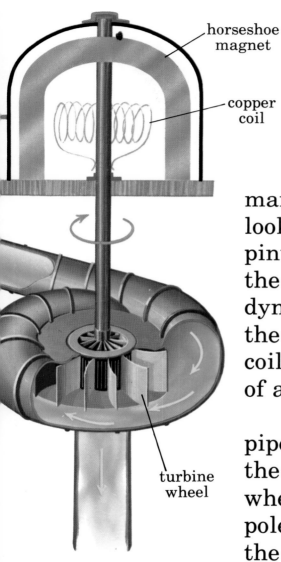

horseshoe
magnet

copper
coil

turbine
wheel

A turbine wheel has many curved blades. It looks a little like a pinwheel. In the middle of the wheel is the pole of a dynamo. At the other end of the pole is a copper coil. The coil is between the two ends of a horseshoe magnet.

The water goes down the pipe so fast that it pushes the blades of the turbine wheel. The blades turn the pole of the dynamo. Then the pole turns the coil. This makes electricity.

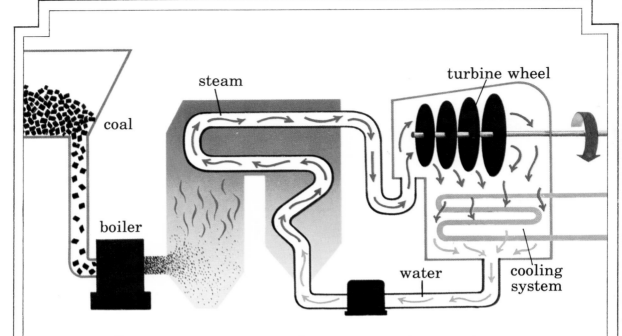

steam

coal

boiler

turbine wheel

water

cooling
system

Some power stations use steam to run a
dynamo. Steam has energy. It can push up
the lid of a teakettle.

A lot of steam can be used to make
electricity. Coal is burned to heat water in
a boiler. The hot water turns into steam.
The steam rushes through a pipe and
pushes the blades on a turbine wheel. The
wheel turns a pole which holds a copper
coil. This makes electricity. The steam is
then cooled and sent back to be heated
up again.

This is a nuclear power station. It uses uranium to make electricity. Uranium is a valuable metal. A small piece of uranium can make a lot of electricity.

Uranium is made of many small pieces called atoms. When uranium atoms break into smaller pieces, there is a lot of heat. The uranium in a nuclear power station is used to boil water. The steam made from the boiling water runs a turbine. The turbine makes electricity.

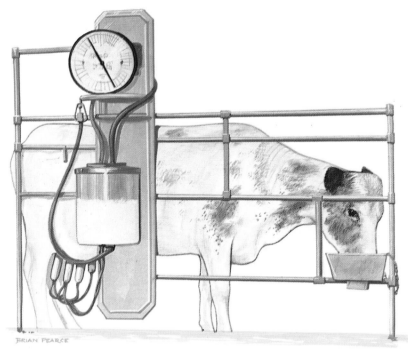

Electricity is used for things all around us. Many offices have electric typewriters. Electricity is also used in factories. Many machines are run by electricity.

Electricity is also used on farms. This cow is being milked by an electric milking machine. Farmers also use electricity for barn heaters. The heaters keep animals warm during the winter.

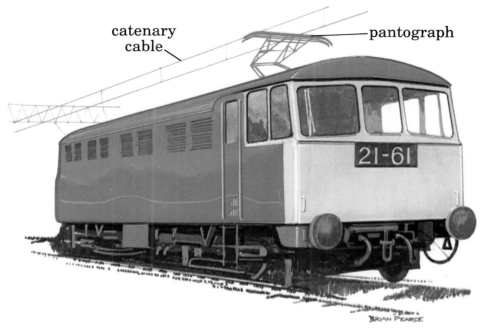

catenary cable

pantograph

21-61

BRIAN PEARCE

Some trains run on electricity. The electricity goes through a special cable. The cable is held over the train tracks by transmission poles. This cable is called a catenary cable. Each train engine has a copper bar on its top. The bar is held against the cable by springs. The bar and springs are called a pantograph. The bar takes electricity from the cable and sends it to the train's engine.

A dynamo isn't the only way to make electricity. Batteries have electricity. There are two kinds of batteries. One is called a dry cell battery. It can make electricity by itself. Portable radios and flashlights run on dry cell batteries.

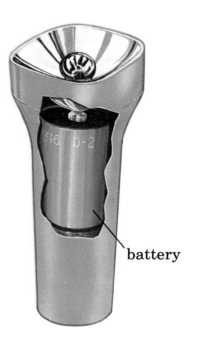

battery

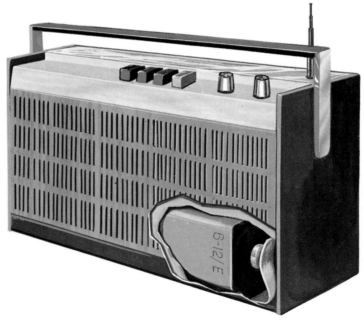

Most dry cell batteries have a case made of zinc. Zinc is a metal. In the middle of the battery is a pole or rod. This rod is made of carbon. Between the carbon and zinc is a chemical. When the carbon and the zinc are connected, electricity is made.

Another kind of dry cell battery is called a solar cell. Each cell is a thin strip of silicon. Silicon comes from sand. On one strip is a metal called arsenic. On another strip is a metal called boron. When light hits the silicon cells, it makes electricity. The electricity then goes to the wire.

A solar battery can work in any strong light. It can use light from the sun.

carbon rod

paste

zinc casing

dry cell battery

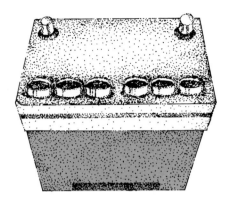

Another kind of battery is a wet cell battery. Another name for a wet cell is a storage battery. A storage battery does not make electricity. It only holds it. Electricity is put in a storage battery by a dynamo. When the battery is used, the electricity goes out of the battery.

Storage batteries are used to start engines of cars and trucks that run on gasoline. Storage batteries can also be used to run cars or trucks. Cars and trucks that run on batteries are slow, but they are much cleaner. They do not make the air dirty.

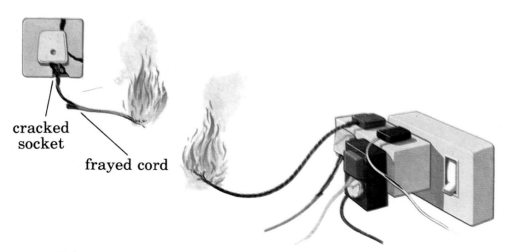

cracked
socket

frayed cord

Electricity does many good things, but it can also be dangerous. Always be careful when you use electricity. Never use a cracked outlet. Never use a frayed or worn-out cord. They can cause fires. Never put too many plugs into one outlet. They can cause fires too.

Electricity and water can be dangerous together. Never touch a switch or outlet when your hands are wet. You may get an electric shock. Electric shocks can kill people.

lightning

Some electricity is in nature. One kind of natural electricity is lightning. Lightning is a big electric spark in the air.

Never stand under a tree during a thunderstorm. Lightning sometimes hits trees and sets them on fire. You could get hurt.

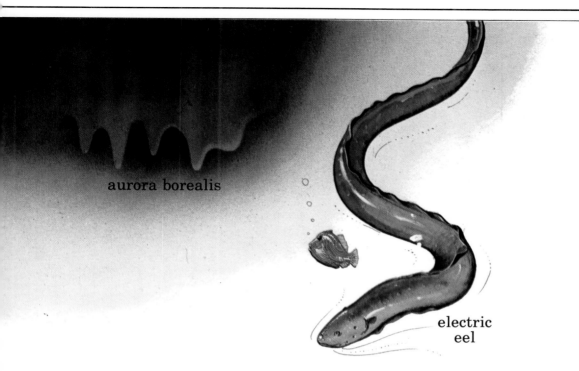

aurora borealis

electric eel

In some parts of the world, people see lights in the sky. One of these places is the far northern part of the world. These lights are called the aurora borealis, or northern lights.

Lights in the sky can also be seen in the far southern part of the world. These lights are called the aurora australis, or southern lights. The northern and southern lights are caused by electricity in the air.

An electric eel catches small fish by giving them electric shocks.

Benjamin Franklin was the first person to find out that lightning is electricity. He flew a kite during a thunderstorm.

key

He put a big key on the kite string. When lightning struck the kite, Franklin touched the key. There was a spark. He got a shock. It was an electric shock.

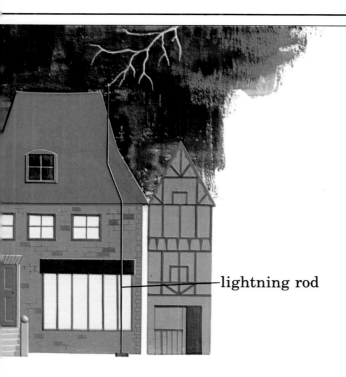

—lightning rod

You shouldn't try Franklin's experiment. It is very dangerous. Franklin almost died from the electric shock.

Lightning can hit tall, pointed buildings. It can set them on fire. Franklin used what he learned about lightning to help stop fires. He invented the lightning rod. It is a long metal rod that is put on top of a house. It goes along the side of the house all the way to the ground. When lightning goes toward the building, it hits the lightning rod instead of the roof. The lightning goes down the rod and into the ground. This is how a lightning rod protects a house from fire.

As people learned more about electricity, they learned how to use it. One of the first ways electricity was used was for sending messages. Samuel Morse invented the telegraph key. The telegraph uses electricity to send messages. When you press the telegraph key, electricity goes through it. When you let it up, the electricity stops.

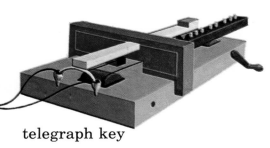

telegraph key

telegraph wires

The electricity goes to wires. The wires take the electricity to where the message is going.

The electricity makes a sound when the key is pressed down. Morse also invented a code for the telegraph. His code had short sounds, called dots. It also had long sounds, called dashes. The dots and dashes were used to spell out words. The telegraph and the code made it easy to send messages a long way in a very short time.

telegraph wire

telegraph key

first light bulb

Another use of electricity was the light
bulb. Joseph Swan made the first electric
light bulb in 1860. It used a carbon rod.
Other people made this light bulb better
and better. Finally, Thomas Edison found a
way to make light bulbs that lasted a
long time and did not cost too much
money to use.

The Metric System

In the United States, things are measured in inches, pounds, quarts, and so on. Most countries of the world use centimeters, kilograms, and liters for these things. The United States uses the American system to measure things. Most other countries use the metric system. By 1985, the United States will be using the metric system, too.

In some books, you will see two systems of measurement. For example, you might see a sentence like this: "That bicycle wheel is 27 inches (69 centimeters) across." When all countries have changed to the metric system, inches will not be used any more. But until then, you may sometimes have to change measurements from one system to the other. The chart on the next page will help you.

All you have to do is multiply the unit of measurement in Column 1 by the number in Column 2. That gives you the unit in Column 3.

Suppose you want to change 5 inches to centimeters. First, find inches in Column 1. Next, multiply 5 times 2.54. You get 12.7. So, 5 inches is 12.7 centimeters.

Column 1	Column 2	Column 3
THIS UNIT OF MEASUREMENT	TIMES THIS NUMBER	GIVES THIS UNIT OF MEASUREMENT
inches	2.54	centimeters
feet	30.	centimeters
feet	.3	meters
yards	.9	meters
miles	1.6	kilometers
ounces	28.	grams
pounds	.45	kilograms
fluid ounces	.03	liters
pints	.47	liters
quarts	.95	liters
gallons	3.8	liters
centimeters	.4	inches
meters	1.1	yards
kilometers	.6	miles
grams	.035	ounces
kilograms	2.2	pounds
liters	33.8	fluid ounces
liters	2.1	pints
liters	1.06	quarts
liters	.26	gallons

Where to Read About
Electricity

northern lights (nôr′ t͟hərn   līts′) *p. 27*
nuclear power (noo̅′ klē ər   pou′ ər) *p. 19*
power station (pou′ ər   stā′ shən) *pp. 13, 16,*
    18, 19
southern lights (sut͟h′ ərn   līts′) *p. 27*
telegraph (tel′ ə graf) *pp. 30-31*
transmission tower (trans mish′ ən   tou′ ər)
    p. 12
turbine wheel (tur′ bin   hwēl′) *p. 17*
uranium (yoo rā′ nē əm) *p. 19*
wet cell (wet′   sel) *p. 24*

Pronunciation Key

a	a as in **cat, bad**
ā	a as in **able,** ai as in **train,** ay as in **play**
ä	a as in **father, car,** o as in **cot**
e	e as in **bend, yet**
ē	e as in **me,** ee as in **feel,** ea as in **beat,** ie as in **piece,** y as in **heavy**
i	i as in **in, pig,** e as in **pocket**
ī	i as in **ice, time,** ie as in **tie,** y as in **my**
o	o as in **top,** a as in **watch**
ō	o as in **old,** oa as in **goat,** ow as in **slow,** oe as in **toe**
ô	o as in **cloth,** au as in **caught,** aw as in **paw,** a as in **all**
oo	oo as in **good,** u as in **put**
o͞o	oo as in **tool,** ue as in **blue**
oi	oi as in **oil,** oy as in **toy**
ou	ou as in **out,** ow as in **plow**
u	u as in **up, gun,** o as in **other**
ur	ur as in **fur,** er as in **person,** ir as in **bird,** or as in **work**
yo͞o	u as in **use,** ew as in **few**
ə	a as in **again,** e as in **broken,** i as in **pencil,** o as in **attention,** u as in **surprise**
ch	ch as in **such**
ng	ng as in **sing**
sh	sh as in **shell, wish**
th	th as in **three, bath**
<u>th</u>	th as in **that, together**

GLOSSARY

These words are defined the way they are used in this book

acid (as′ id) a chemical used in storage batteries

aluminum (ə loo′ mə nəm) a metal used to make conduits

ammonium chloride (ə mon′ ē əm klor′ īd) a chemical; the paste used in dry cell batteries

arsenic (är′ sə nik) a metal used in silicon cells

atom (at′ əm) a small piece of matter

bar magnet (bär mag′ nət) a piece of metal that can be used to make a dynamo

barn heater (bärn′ hē′ tər) a heater used by farmers to keep animals warm in the winter

battery (bat′ ər ē) something that can make or store electricity

boil (boil) to make very hot; water can be boiled to make steam

boiler (boi′ lər) a device used to boil water

boron (bōr′ on) a metal used in silicon cells

build (bild) to make or put together

cable (kā′ bəl) a thick wire; cables are used to bring electricity to your house

carbon (kär′ bən) a material used in some dry cell batteries

casing (kā′ sing) the outside part of a dry cell battery

catenary cable (kat′ ə ner ē kā′ bəl) the cable that brings electricity to electric trains

cell (sel) a small piece of something; a battery is made up of cells that make electricity

chemical (kem′ ə kəl) a kind of substance sometimes used in batteries

click (klik) one kind of sound used in Morse code

coal (kōl) a kind of fuel used in some power stations to make electricity

code (kōd) a language; Morse code is a
language

conductor (kən duk′ tər) something
that carries electricity; a lightning
conductor protects houses from
lightning by taking it away from the house

conduit (kän′ do͞o ət) a metal pipe that
holds the electrical wires that are in a
house's walls

connect (kə nekt′) to bring two or more
things together

copper coil (kop′ ər koil′) a curved,
twisted piece of copper metal used in a
dynamo

cord (kôrd) a protected wire used to
bring electricity to an appliance

crack (krak) a split or break

curve (kurv) a line or edge that has a bend
in it; a turbine wheel has a curved edge

dam (dam) something that holds back
water

dash (dash) one of the sounds used in
Morse code

discharge (dis′ chärj) to use up; when the electricity in a storage battery is being used up, the battery is discharging

distribution transformer (dis′ trə byoo′ shən trans fôr′ mər) something used to bring electricity from a power station

dot (dät) one of the clicks used in Morse code

dynamo (dī′ nə mō′) a machine that makes electricity

electric (i lek′ trik) using or involving electricity

electricity (i lek tris′ ə tē) energy used to run machines and appliances

energy (en′ ər jē) power

engine (en′ jin) a machine that makes energy and is used to run another machine

experiment (eks per′ ə mənt) a test or trial

factory (fak′ tər ē) a place where things are made

farm (färm) a place where people grow food and raise animals

filament (fil′ ə mənt) the thin metal strip inside a light bulb

fluorescent light (floor es′ ənt līt′) a kind of gas discharge lamp

fray (frā) to wear out; a frayed cord is worn out and dangerous

gas discharge lamp (gas dis′ chärj lamp) a light bulb or lamp that makes light by using gas and electricity

glow (glō) to shine with a bright light

heat (hēt) warmth

horseshoe magnet (hôrs′ shoo mag′ nət) a piece of metal shaped like a horseshoe that can attract other metals; it can be used in a dynamo

hydro (hī′ drō) a word that means water

hydroelectricity (hī′ drō i lek tris′ ə tē) electricity made by water

invent (ən vent′) to make something new, such as a machine or tool

kite (kīt) an object made of wood, paper, and string that flies in the air.

Benjamin Franklin used a kite to learn about lightning.

lamp (lamp) something that holds a light bulb

language (lang' gwij) what people use to speak or communicate with each other

lead (led) a metal used in storage batteries

lid (lid) the movable cover of a container

lightning (līt' ning) a big electric spark that appears in the sky during thunderstorms

lightning rod (līt' ning rod') a long, round piece of metal that is put on buildings to protect them from lightning

magnet (mag' nət) a piece of metal that has electricity in it

main (mān) most important

message (mes' ij) words sent from one person to another

metal (met' əl) an element that can conduct electricity

meter (mē' tər) the machine that measures

the electricity that goes into a building

nature (nā′ chər) the world around us

nuclear power (noo′ klē ər pou′ ər)
  electricity made at a nuclear power station

office (ô′ fis) a place where people work

ordinary (ôrd′ ən er′ ē) normal or
  regular or average

outlet (out′ let) where a cord can be
  plugged in to get electricity

overhead (ō′ vər hed′) above; overhead
  lamps are attached to the ceiling or
  high on a wall

pantagraph (pant′ ə graf) the copper
  bar on an electric train that takes
  electricity from the catenary cable to
  the train's engine

paste (pāst) a thick substance; paste in a
  dry cell separates the zinc and boron in
  a battery

pipe (pīp) a round piece of metal used to
  hold electric wires

plug (plug) the end of the cord of a lamp
  that is put into an electric outlet

portable (pôr′ tə bəl) able to be carried around

power station (pou′ ər stā shən) a place where electricity is made

press (pres) to push out or down

reactor (rē ak′ tər) the case that holds uranium in a nuclear power station

rod (rod) a pole; usually a long piece of metal

sand (sand) a substance used to make silicon cells

shock (shok) a pain; an electric shock is a strong, sudden pain caused by electricity

silicon (sil′ ə kən) a substance that comes from sand; it is used in solar batteries

silicon cell (sil′ i kən sel′) a dry cell that makes electricity from sunlight or some other strong light

socket (säk′ it) outlet; a place to get electricity

solar battery (sō′ lər bat′ ər ē) a battery that can make electricity from sunlight or other strong light. It is made of silicon cells.

spark (spärk) a flash of electricity

spring (spring) a piece of metal that is wound in a circle

steam (stēm) the vapor that is formed when water is boiled

steel (stēl) a metal

storage battery (stôr′ ij bat′ ər ē) a battery that holds electricity. It is made of wet cells.

strip (strip) a long, thin piece of something

switch (swich) something used to turn electricity on or off

teakettle (tē′ ket əl) an appliance used to boil water

telegraph (tel′ ə graf) a machine for sending messages; invented by Samuel Morse

thunderstorm (thun′ dər stôrm′) a storm that has lots of rain, thunder, and lightning

tool (to͞ol) something that can be used to do work

transmission pole (trans mish′ ən pōl′) what is used to carry electric cables from a power station

transmitter (trans mit′ ər) a machine used to send something from one place to another

turbine wheel (tur′ bin hwēl′) a curved wheel used in power generators to make electricity

typewriter (tīp′ rīt ər) a machine used to make letters and words on a piece of paper

uranium (yoo rā′ nē əm) a valuable metal used to make electricity in nuclear power stations

valuable (val′ yoo ə bəl) costing a lot of money; important

worn out (wôrn out) used up; no longer good to be used

zinc (zingk) a metal used in a dry cell battery

Bibliography

Asimov, Isaac. *How Did We Find Out About Electricity?* New York: Walker and Co., 1973.

Barker, Eric J., and Millard, W. F. *Machines and Energy*. New York: Arco Publishing Co., Inc., 1972.

Grey, Jerry. *The Race for Electric Power*. Philadelphia: Westminster Press, 1972.

McCaig, Robert. *Electric Power in America*. New York: G. P. Putnam's Sons, 1970.

Stone, A., and Siegel, B. *Turned On: A Look at Electricity*. Englewood Cliffs, N.J.: Prentice-Hall.